CRACKING THE CODE

BRINGING TO LIGHT THE REAL ESTATE REVOLUTION OF VIRTUAL WHOLESALING

CAROLINE S. CRAFT

Cracking the Code:
Bringing to Light the Real Estate Revolution of Virtual Wholesaling

Caroline S. Craft

Chapter 1: Introduction to Virtual Wholesaling

Introduction: The Virtual Wholesaling Revolution: Unveiling the Future of Real Estate Profits

Greetings from the vanguard of real estate innovation! A new area of real estate investing has evolved in an age where technology helps close the gap between opportunity and execution: virtual wholesaling. The days of limiting your activities to your local market are long gone. Accept a world where profit has no bounds, where trade is worldwide, and where borders are imaginary.

Imagine managing real estate transactions from the comfort of your home, without regard to distance. Thanks to the boundless possibilities of virtual wholesaling, it is now possible to transform properties from undervalued diamonds into lucrative treasures.

We shall go on a journey that goes beyond customary real estate procedures in the chapters that follow. We'll look at how virtual wholesaling is changing the regulations, redefining approaches to the market, and reviving investors like you. Utilizing technology is important, but adopting a mindset that will enable you to succeed in a constantly changing environment is also important.

You'll learn the tricks to spotting off-market opportunities from around the world, negotiating contracts without being present in person, and coordinating smooth remote transactions as we navigate the ins and outs of virtual wholesaling. We'll delve into the art of remote due diligence and expose the tactics used by clever investors to adjust, prosper, and grow their businesses in this new virtual frontier.

Get ready to realize your real estate goals to the fullest. The tools, tactics, and insights included inside these pages will give you the power to achieve success that has no bounds, whether you are an experienced investor looking for fresh opportunities or a beginner eager to get into the market.

Real estate wholesaling's virtual future is already here. Do you have the motivation to change the way you think about investing?

Let's embark on this journey that will change our lives together.

Thank you for visiting the era of real estate gains.

- ## The Concept of Virtual Wholesaling

The Idea of Virtual Wholesaling: Exploring Profit Abroad

A revolution has emerged in the throbbing center of the real estate market, one that transcends boundaries of space, reimagines established paradigms, and unlocks a vast array of unrealized potential. Virtual Wholesaling, a notion that has sparked a blaze of excitement, interest, and promise within the world of real estate investing, is this revolutionary force.

Imagine yourself as a real estate investor who is not constrained by the boundaries of your local market. Imagine being able to coordinate transactions, make agreements, and sign documents all from the comfort of your home. This is the fundamental idea behind virtual wholesaling, a ground-breaking strategy that has enabled investors to prosper on a global scale.

The Virtual Wholesaling Phenomenon: A Breakdown

Virtual wholesaling is fundamentally about embracing a digital environment where opportunities are limitless while overcoming the restrictions of physical location. Finding distressed properties, securing them under contract at a reduced price, and then assigning the contract to another investor in exchange for a fee are all part of traditional real estate wholesaling. The brilliance of virtual wholesaling, however, resides in carrying out these actions without ever setting foot on the real estate.

Why Online Wholesaling Is Important

It's not only a question of why virtual wholesaling matters in a time of connectivity, data accessibility, and rapid technological advancements—it's also a question of why it's become an essential investment strategy for aspirational investors. This is why:

1: Broadening Your Perspectives The boundaries of your local market are broken by virtual wholesaling. You are not limited to homes that are accessible by car. Instead, the entire world serves as your market.

Imagine being able to enter attractive markets that were previously thought to be inaccessible. With virtual wholesaling, you have the ability to look for emerging markets with a lot of promise, regardless of how far away they are from you.

3. Simplifying Operations: Conventional wholesaling can take a lot of time and resources. By streamlining your operations, virtual wholesaling enables you to concentrate on growing your business rather than avoiding traffic.

4: Unlocking Efficiency: You can evaluate properties, carry out due diligence, and negotiate contracts all from the comfort of your office with the right tools and techniques.

5: Risk Reduction: Virtual wholesaling promotes thorough investigation and analysis. You're more inclined to base your selections on thorough facts rather than relying just on local market trends.

Developing Your Online Wholesaling Plan

Entering the virtual wholesale market requires a calculated strategy that blends creativity and thorough planning. Here are some of the important factors to take into account:

1. Conduct market research to better grasp the dynamics of the markets you're aiming at. To make wise judgments, research nearby areas, property values, and societal trends.

2: Leveraging Technology: Adopt technological tools that enable remote property tours, virtual property analysis, and safe document sharing. Your allies include tools for property analysis, virtual reality, and video conferences.

3. Establishing a Reliable Remote Team: Although virtual wholesaling lessens the requirement for physical presence, it increases the significance of an effective remote team. Real estate brokers, builders, and other local

specialists who can offer information you couldn't get from a distance fall under this category.

4: Bargaining Skills: It's essential to master the art of virtual bargaining. You will close transactions using effective communication, assertiveness, and adaptability as your compass.

5: Unleashing Due Diligence Without physically seeing the property, virtual due diligence includes examining property specifics, legal documentation, and market trends. It involves how to use data as a detective and to your benefit.

Getting Around Obstacles and Embracing Innovations

Virtual wholesaling has obstacles, much like any avant-garde idea. The absence of a physical presence, potential misrepresentation of properties, and communication limitations are challenges to overcome. However, these difficulties have stimulated the creation of novel solutions:

1: Advanced Data Analytics: Tools for real-time data and predictive analytics offer insights into market patterns, possible investment returns, and property valuations.

2: Virtual Reality Tours: Using VR technology, investors may remotely tour properties to get a full sense of the layout and condition.

3. Blockchain technology and smart contracts: Smart contracts increase the efficiency, security, and transparency of digital transactions, making remote contracting safer.

Accept the Frontier of Virtual Wholesaling

The idea of virtual wholesaling is no longer just a pipe dream; it is already a reality that is changing the real estate investing landscape. It's an invitation to use technology, data, and creativity to take your business to previously unthinkable heights.

We'll go deeper into the complexities of virtual wholesaling in the succeeding chapters, revealing tactics, success tales, and practical advice. As you set out on this journey, keep in mind that the future of real estate investing rests at the nexus of creativity and aspiration, where virtual wholesaling serves as the link between the potential of today and the wealth of tomorrow.

Get ready to enter a world where finding properties involves clicking, signing contracts involves typing, and money is made by pixels going into your pocket. Welcome to the Virtual Wholesaling era, where the rules are being rewritten rather than merely the game changing.

- **Advantages and Challenges of Virtual Wholesaling**

Discovering the Benefits, Challenges, and Best Practices of Virtual Wholesaling: A Mastering of the Art

A game-changing trend has evolved in the dynamic world of real estate, rewriting the rules of participation and igniting a fresh flurry of interest among investors. Enter Virtual Wholesaling, a paradigm-shifting strategy that is upending conventional real estate practices and paving the way for a revolution in the ways that properties are purchased, sold, and profited from.

The Benefits of Online Wholesaling

1: **International Reach, Local Expertise: Being able to reach markets outside of your own area is one of the most attractive benefits of virtual wholesaling. For the best bargain selection, you can use your local market experience while sourcing discounts from rising hotspots across the nation or even outside.

2. Access to Untapped Opportunities: Through virtual wholesale, you can discover opportunities that may have gone undiscovered in your local market. A broader perspective allows you to find undervalued properties with lots of promise and make money off of them before others do.

3: Operational Efficiency: Conventional real estate activities can include spending a lot of time and money traveling to properties, seeing them, and attending meetings there. These procedures are streamlined by virtual wholesaling, which lets you evaluate deals, hold negotiations, and complete transactions from the convenience of your office.

4. Scalability: Growing physical operations is typically required to scale a real estate business, which can be difficult. On the other hand, virtual wholesaling naturally lends itself to growth. Once you've created efficient virtual workflows, expanding your business just requires copying your winning tactics in other marketplaces.

5: Data-Driven Decision Making: Data analytics are the lifeblood of virtual wholesaling. Real-time market information, property valuations, neighborhood trends, and more are all available to you. You can use this information to create decisions that are supported by knowledge rather than speculation.

6: Flexibility and Freedom: One distinguishing benefit of virtual wholesaling is the freedom to conduct business from any location. You may work actively on your business whether you're in a busy city or a secluded lodge, and you have the freedom to organize your time anyway you like.

Issues with Virtual Wholesaling

1: Effective communication is crucial in the real estate industry, and virtual wholesaling presents its own set of difficulties. Building rapport remotely and misinterpreting intentions and details can be challenging.

2: Authenticating the Property: Relying entirely on internet listings and data may result in misunderstandings regarding the state of the property. You run the risk of overlooking significant information that could affect your investing choice if you don't actually see the property.

3: Local Knowledge: If you are not physically present in a market, you risk missing out on the complex market knowledge that local investors have. These revelations might affect real estate appraisals, remodeling choices, and even negotiation tactics.

4: Document Security and Legal Compliance: To prevent data breaches, managing contracts, agreements, and sensitive information in a virtual environment calls for rigorous security measures. Understanding the legal peculiarities in various markets also becomes essential to maintaining compliance.

5: Creating Relationships: In the real estate sector, face-to-face interactions are crucial to creating relationships based on trust. Similar connections can be made virtually, but it might take more time and effort.

Guidelines for Effective Virtual Wholesaling

1: Prioritize communication as a first step in order to reduce problems with it. Create open lines of communication. To promote effective cooperation, use video conferencing, instant messaging, and frequent check-ins with your distant workforce.

2: Comprehensive Virtual Due Diligence: Take the time to conduct thorough virtual due diligence. Utilize technology to evaluate neighborhood patterns, determine property values, and learn as much as you can about the properties you are contemplating.

3: Utilize local partnerships to gather knowledge that might not be easily accessible online. Work with neighborhood contractors, property managers, and real estate brokers. These collaborations may offer priceless local expertise.

4: Virtual Property Tours: Make use of virtual reality (VR) technology to give prospective buyers virtual tours of properties. This bridges the gap between online listings and in-person visits by enabling them to experience the property remotely.

5: Implement strong security protocols to safeguard sensitive data. Secure digital infrastructure. Consider using blockchain for safe contract administration and using encrypted communication tools and secure document sharing sites.

6: Keep up on market developments, technical innovations, and the best practices for virtual wholesaling. Adapt your plans in light of fresh information and new resources.

Conclusion: Real estate investment's future

Virtual wholesaling is a paradigm change that is changing the real estate investing landscape, not a passing fad. It offers an unrivaled chance to use innovation, data, and technology to drive profits across borders. You put yourself in a position to lead this transformational movement by making the most of the benefits, overcoming the difficulties, and adopting best practices.

It's important to keep in mind that success in virtual wholesaling requires a combination of technological prowess with strategic thought, rigorous research, and a dedication to forging deep connections in a digital world. You're not just navigating the difficulties as you start your adventure into virtual wholesaling; you're also paving the way for the real estate investing of the future, where the opportunities are only limited by your desire.

Chapter 2: Getting Started with Virtual Wholesaling

Your Guide to Getting Started in the Virtual Wholesaling Odyssey

A new star has emerged in the constantly changing world of real estate investment: the phenomenon of virtual wholesaling. This ground-breaking method goes beyond the restrictions of physical distance, allowing access to previously imagined prospects. Fasten your seatbelt as we walk you through the thrilling process of beginning virtual wholesaling if you're prepared to enter this virtual world.

The Way to Master Virtual Wholesaling

Setting Sail for Unknown Regions

Imagine a world in which your ability to make wise investments is not constrained by your immediate surroundings. Imagine yourself working comfortably in your own workspace while finding bargains, analyzing properties, and finalizing deals. Welcome to the center of virtual wholesaling, where creativity, technology, and strategy converge to reimagine the fundamentals of real estate enterprise.

The Initial Steps: Building the Base

1: Develop Your Strategy First: Clarify your objectives first. Are you looking to expand into new areas, increase the size of your business, or just streamline your current operations? You will navigate this virtual journey with a clear plan.

2. Pick Your Markets: Here, research can be an ally. Find markets that support your objectives and exhibit potential for growth and demand. Property valuations, rental yields, and economic stability are important considerations.

3. Create Your Virtual Team: While the requirement for a physical presence is reduced with virtual wholesaling, the value of a great virtual team is increased. You'll probably need real estate brokers, home inspectors, contractors, and local specialists who can offer perceptions that can only come from first-hand experience.

4: Invest in technology: Take advantage of the gadgets that will complete your digital toolbox. The key elements are real estate analytic software, virtual reality platforms for remote property tours, and long-distance communication technologies.

The Influence of Networking and Market Research

1: Conduct thorough research into the markets you have selected. Examine the past figures, current trends in development, employment rates, and local features. To obtain important information, make use of web tools, market reports, and discussion forums.

2. Networking in the Digital Age: Even in a virtual environment, developing relationships is crucial. Engage on social media, attend virtual meetups, join online real estate communities, and make connections with regional experts who can offer priceless insights.

Developing Your Deal-Finding Plan

1: Make Use of Online Resources: Profit from online resources that focus on off-market properties. You can find hidden treasures that typical investors might overlook using websites, databases, and listing services.

2. Direct Marketing Campaigns: Create persuasive marketing plans that directly contact potential sellers. Lead generation that meets your investment criteria can be achieved through email marketing, social media ads, and focused outreach.

Property Evaluation in a Virtual Environment

Utilize technology to examine properties remotely in step one of the analysis process. Use software for property analysis to examine possible returns, predict repair costs, and assess a deal's viability.

Despite the fact that you might not be able to physically enter a place, technology provides alternatives. You may get a complete picture of the property's condition through virtual reality tours and video chats with local partners.

Remote Contracting and Negotiation

1: Developing Virtual Negotiation Skills: Deals must be negotiated virtually, which calls for strong communication abilities. Be sure to actively listen, comprehend the seller's intentions, and express your terms in detail.

2: Secure digital platforms for contract signing offer ease and security. Learn how to use e-signature software, and make sure you understand the legal requirements for remote contracting.

Conducting Due Diligence and Virtual Closing

1. Thorough virtual due diligence Whether it is done in person or virtually, careful due diligence is essential. Verify property information, evaluate title information, and learn about local laws by using online resources.

2. Coordinate distant transactions by partnering with a title business that provides virtual closing services. Make sure every financial and legal consideration is carefully considered.

Best Practices for Starting a Virtual Wholesaling Business

1: Continuous Learning: The virtual wholesale market is a dynamic one. To keep your competitive edge, keep up with market trends, emerging technologies, and technological developments.

2. Begin modestly and expand: Start by conducting controlled tests of your strategies. Scale your operations to new markets or more transaction flow once you've polished your strategy and earned confidence.

3. Flexibility: Flexibility is necessary for virtual wholesaling. Be ready to adjust your strategies in response to market fluctuations, team input, and changing customer demands.

4: Communication Prowess: Master numerous communication venues to overcome communication obstacles. The key to success is open, regular, and succinct communication with your staff and partners.

The Beginning of Your Online Wholesaling Odyssey

As you start along the road of virtual wholesaling, keep in mind that success depends on your readiness to change, pick up new skills, and seize the chances that technology and innovation present. A plan that is in line with your goals, the development of meaningful relationships, and the ability to make decisions even when you are miles away from the property are all important components of virtual wholesaling.

The virtual world beckons, promising fresh perspectives and unrealized possibilities. You're prepared to make a name for yourself in the field of virtual wholesaling by having a strong foundation, conducting thorough research, and making a commitment to always being on the cutting edge. The journey you're on has only just begun; get ready for the adventure that awaits.

• Building Your Virtual Wholesaling Strategy

Building a Successful Virtual Wholesaling Strategy with Crafting Triumph

A new era has begun in the fascinating field of real estate, one marked by a digital symphony of creativity, tact, and ground-breaking potential. Virtual Wholesaling, a dynamic strategy that is luring investors into a world where properties are surveyed, agreements are closed, and profits are increased, all inside the embrace of a virtual landscape, is the source of this fascinating phenomenon.

Using a Virtual Wholesaling Strategy to Navigate the World

Finding a Route to Online Prosperity

Imagine having a global investment platform where you aren't constrained by physical boundaries. Imagine managing transactions, examining properties, and creating success tales all from the convenience of your chosen location. We cordially invite you to join us in the world of virtual wholesaling, where technology and business acumen combine to redefine the fundamentals of real estate enterprise.

Developing Your Blueprint for Virtual Wholesaling

The Foundation for Strategic Excellence

1. Identify Your Special Approach: A clearly defined approach is the first step on your journey. Do you want to take advantage of emerging markets? Or maybe you want to scale your business across regions? Describe your objectives so that you can adjust your plan.

2: Market Selection Mastery: Invest heavily in market research. Analyze regional trends, property values, and growth potential. The foundation of the success of your approach will be this understanding.

The value of your virtual workforce is highlighted by virtual wholesaling, which reduces the requirement for physical presence. Work together with local specialists who can offer perceptions from the ground, such as real estate brokers, builders, property managers, and contractors.

4: Adopt Technology's Arsenal: Arm yourself with the necessary implements. Your virtual arsenal must include tools for real estate analysis, virtual reality platforms for property tours, and distance-bridging communication apps.

Unveiling of the Virtual Wholesaling Strategy

Deal discovery and property analysis techniques

1: Digital Deal Discovery: Make use of web tools for finding off-market assets. Discover hidden treasures by exploring specialist websites, databases, and listing services.

2: Direct Marketing Finesse: Create persuasive marketing efforts that speak directly to motivated sellers. To connect with potential leads, create appealing email campaigns, interesting social media ads, and personalized outreach.

3: Utilize technology to analyze properties effectively in step three. Software for property analysis offers information on possible returns, maintenance costs, and overall investment viability.

4: With virtual reality property tours, you can fully immerse yourself in the future. This technology bridges the gap between online listings and in-person visits by giving potential buyers an authentic sense for a property.

Contracting and Bargaining in the Digital World

Building Your Skills in Contracting and Negotiation

1: The first principle of virtual negotiating is that effective communication is essential. Master the skill of active listening, comprehend the drivers behind vendors, and skillfully communicate your demands.

2: Excellence in Digital Contracting: Explore the world of safe digital contracting platforms. Learn how to use e-signature software, and make sure you understand the legal requirements for remote contracting.

Complete Due Diligence and Quick Closings

Almost perfect from due diligence through closing

1: Exemplary virtual due diligence is the cornerstone of successful virtual wholesaling. Examine title information, confirm property specifics, and thoroughly explore local laws using online resources.

2: Seamless Virtual Closings: Collaborate with a title agency with a focus on online closings. Accurately navigate the difficulties of distant transactions while making sure that all monetary and legal considerations are taken into account.

Guidelines for a Successful Virtual Wholesaling Strategy

Improve Your Strategy with Proven Techniques

1: Support Continuous Learning: Information is key in the dynamic world of virtual wholesaling. To keep your competitive edge, keep up with market trends, emerging technologies, and technical developments.

2: Start Small, Scale Smart: Test your strategies in a safe setting to start your trip. Increase your deal flow or broaden your reach to other markets once you've perfected your strategy and earned confidence.

3. Flexibility is a virtue: The virtual world is dynamic, therefore be ready to adjust your strategies in response to changes in the market, team feedback, and your company's changing needs.

4: Champion Communication: Masterfully navigate communication difficulties. Your success in virtual wholesaling rests on your ability to communicate with your team and partners clearly, consistently, and concisely.

Building a virtual wholesaling strategy has several advantages.

1: Local knowledge with a global reach: Your plan acts as a road map for growing your audience while utilizing your knowledge of the local market. By fine-tuning your technique, you may access marketplaces outside of your immediate area, giving you the ability to find deals with accuracy and wisdom.

2: Enhanced Efficiency Your activities are optimized by a well-designed strategy. You are no longer restricted by tiresome property visits or drawn-out commutes. By concentrating your efforts on assessing, negotiating, and closing deals, your strategy streamlines your efforts.

3. Scale with Confidence: Scalable growth is built on a solid virtual wholesaling strategy. You may easily enter new markets and increase your reach as you refine your strategy and copy effective ones.

4: Data-Driven Decisions: Your approach depends on data analysis and market research. With knowledge of market conditions, local trends, and property values, you are equipped to make judgments that will contribute to your success.

5: Developing a strategy for virtual wholesaling gives you the flexibility to work from any location. Your workstation is no longer limited to a physical location; instead, it can be located wherever you like.

Final Thoughts: Your Online Wholesale Odyssey Awaits

Take advantage of the chance to combine creativity, strategy, and technology as you start your virtual wholesaling career. Create a roadmap that supports your goals, establish connections, even online, and take wise decisions that cut across boundaries.

You are being called to pave the way in the field of virtual wholesaling by the future of real estate investing. You are prepared to write your own success story if you have a strong foundation, persistent commitment, and a dash of creativity. Enter this exciting voyage where fortunes are made in codes and assets are swapped for pixels. Begin your voyage right away, and enjoy the adventure that lies ahead.

• Setting Up Your Remote Wholesaling Team

Building Your Remote Wholesaling Dream Team with the Architects of Success

A new phenomena has emerged in the field of real estate, where strategy and innovation are intertwined: a remote wholesaling dream team that transcends geographical boundaries and fosters success. Remote Wholesaling Teams, dynamic groups of experts who work electronically to plan transactions, assess properties, and maximize profitability, are this force's magnet. Join us as we explore the strategies, advantages, and best practices that will help you succeed as we unravel the fascinating adventure of putting up your remote wholesaling team.

Putting Together the Ultimate Virtual Team: Your Remote Wholesaling Team

The Start of Efficient Virtual Success

Imagine a situation in which geographic distances become irrelevant and professionals from all over the world come together to build a formidable team that thrives on cooperation, invention, and expertise. A remote wholesaling dream team has this kind of synergy, which turns real estate investing into an online masterpiece.

An advantage of a remote wholesale team is:

1. Expanded knowledge: By utilizing a varied range of abilities and insights, a remote wholesaling team increases your knowledge. With a network of experts offering their specific

knowledge, you are no longer constrained by your own understanding.

2: Increased Efficiency: Virtual cooperation does not require physical proximity. Individual task completion allows your team members to focus and use their time more efficiently. A quicker deal close and higher productivity result from this improved efficiency.

3. Global Market Mastery: You can obtain first-hand expertise of many markets by assembling a team from various geographical areas. You can spot possibilities, trends, and potential problems that you might have overlooked without this global perspective.

4: Scale Effortlessly: As your business grows, your remote workforce may easily transfer profitable business models to other markets. Growing your company becomes a strategic process as opposed to an operational difficulty.

Developing a Blueprint for Your Remote Wholesaling Team

Creating a Virtual Synergy Strategy

1: Define Your Team Roles in Step 1: Outline the roles that are necessary for your remote team to start. Real estate agents, property analysts, contractors, title specialists, and administrative assistance should all be taken into consideration.

2: Utilize the power of the internet to uncover talent outside of your immediate network in step two, global talent search. To find possible team members, use freelance platforms, specialist real estate forums, and business networking websites.

3. Cultural awareness is essential when putting together a remote team. Different geographical areas have distinctive customs, laws, and communication patterns. The cultural variety of your team should be a source of strength rather than conflict.

4: Establish clear routes of communication to demonstrate communication mastery. To keep everyone on the same page and informed, use tools like video conferencing, messaging applications, and project management software.

Strategies for Team Collaboration in Remote Wholesaling

Disclosing the Techniques for Successful Virtual Collaboration

1: Make sure that everyone on your team is on the same page with your main objectives by setting unified goals. This transparency makes sure that everyone's efforts are directed toward reaching the same goals.

2. Hold frequent virtual gatherings to promote a spirit of cooperation and fellowship. These gatherings provide a forum for exchanging ideas, debating tactics, and dealing with problems.

3: Project Management Tools Adopt project management tools to assign work, monitor deadlines, and track progress. These tools facilitate teamwork and maintain accountability.

4. Transparent Data Sharing: Openly share information and ideas. This open method promotes creativity and empowers team members to make wise choices.

Best Practices for Increasing the Potential of Remote Teams

Release Your Virtual Ensemble's Full Potential

- Despite the virtual aspect of your team, relationship-building should be given priority. A sense of community is fostered through frequent check-ins, virtual team-building exercises, and milestone celebrations.

- Establish roles, duties, and expectations for each team member in clear terms. This transparency avoids misconceptions and guarantees that everyone is aware of their role in the team's success.

- Investment in continual training and skill development for your remote employees is step three. Giving team members room to grow keeps them engaged and increases their contribution to your business.

Finally, Your Remote Wholesaling Dream Team is Here!

As you enter the world of remote wholesaling teams, keep in mind that the key to success is teamwork, effective communication, and utilizing a global network of experts. Carefully craft your strategy, select your team, and harness the power of virtual synergy. The advantages are endless, including the opportunity to scale your firm beyond your wildest dreams and the expertise of a global network.

Real estate investing is going global, going virtual, and going collaborative. You are paving the way for a new era of real estate success with a remote wholesaling dream team by your side, one that thrives on innovation, strategy, and the practice of virtual collaboration. Welcome to the world where connections are made through keystrokes, dreams are achieved through pixels, and success has no boundaries. Your path to virtual victory starts right now.

Chapter 3: Finding and Analyzing Virtual Deals

Finding and Examining Deals on Virtual Real Estate on the Digital Terrain

A seismic shift is taking place in the constantly changing world of real estate investing, one that questions established conventions, transcends geographical boundaries, and transforms the way buyers find and assess homes. This paradigm change is brought about by the art of locating and evaluating virtual real estate deals—a paradigm that makes use of digital resources, allows investors to explore various markets from a distance, and improves the accuracy of property assessments. Join us on an educational adventure as we explore the complex world of locating and evaluating virtual real estate deals, reveal successful tactics, and reveal the procedures that result in resounding success.

Finding and analyzing virtual deals as you embark on your digital quest

Discovering the Core of Virtual Deals

Imagine a scenario in which geographic restrictions no longer limit your capacity to spot intriguing real estate prospects. In this scenario, technology serves as your portal for investigating assets and markets from any location in the world. Imagine a world where due diligence is completed remotely, allowing you to evaluate the possibilities of properties without ever having to step foot on the real property. This is the area of discovering and evaluating virtual real estate bargains; it's a setting where inventiveness and business acumen combine to transform the discovery and assessment of agreements.

How to Find Deals on Virtual Real Estate

- Online listing services Explore the wealth of real estate listings that are available online. These websites display a variety of properties, each with thorough information, high-quality photos, and occasionally even virtual tours.

- Digital networking: Make use of social media sites, real estate discussion boards, and online groups to interact with other investors, real estate experts, and potential business partners who can give you useful leads on off-market prospects.

- Direct Outreach: Use the power of internet communication to get in touch with potential buyers directly, such as property owners. You can indicate your interest in their properties by sending them emails, social media messages, and messaging through virtual gatherings.
- Join online platforms and networks for virtual wholesaling, which help buyers and sellers connect with each other. These platforms frequently compile a list of investment opportunities, speeding up the transaction discovery process.

- Deals in virtual real estate analysis: thorough data Utilize the abundance of online data sources to compile crucial information about market trends, rental rates, property prices, and comparable transactions. You are given the knowledge necessary to evaluate the possibilities of a deal thanks to our data-driven methodology.

- Utilize resources such as satellite images, internet mapping services, and property management software to remotely evaluate a property's state, location, and potential for future development.

- Detailed financial models that forecast possible cash flows, return on investment (ROI), and other important financial metrics can be created using spreadsheet software. The profitability of a deal can be clearly understood using this analytical approach.

- Conduct complete due diligence duties, such as title searches, property inspections, and tenant verifications, by hiring virtual assistants, local experts, or property management firms.

Successful Deal Discovery and Analysis Techniques:

- Create a Strong Online Presence: Develop a credible online identity through social media, individual websites, and forum participation related to real estate. This not only displays your knowledge but also draws potential business partners.

- Employ digital marketing techniques to immediately contact potential sellers with your targeted marketing initiatives. Effective outcomes in deal sourcing can be achieved by creating engaging messages and using targeted advertising.

- Embrace networking by actively taking part in online forums, webinars, and conferences related to real estate. By networking, you can find significant mentors, partners, and investment opportunities.

- Making Use of Technological Tools Include technologies and resources that speed up the transaction analysis and discovery process. Platforms for aggregating data and automating procedures can greatly increase productivity.

Overcoming Obstacles in Virtual Deal Analysis and Discovery:

- Market knowledge: In-depth study is necessary to navigate uncharted marketplaces. To fill the information gap, rely on web resources, market studies, and the opinions of local experts.

- Verify the accuracy of data obtained from reputable platforms to ensure that your analyses are founded on current, dependable facts.

- Authenticity of a virtual asset: Although useful, virtual evaluations cannot match the depth of real checks. For thorough property evaluations, rely on neighborhood resources, virtual assistants, or property management companies.

- Creating Trust Online: In a virtual setting, building confidence with sellers and partners necessitates excellent communication, transparency, and professionalism.

Final Thoughts: Exploring the Digital Frontier of Deal Analysis

Remember that technology is your compass, strategy is your guide, and adaptation is your power as you reach the end of this voyage. Accept the benefits of global deal sourcing, make the most of digital tools, and navigate the digital environment with skill.

You are at the forefront of a shift in real estate investing that is taking place via internet platforms, data-driven analytics, and pixels. You are well-positioned to succeed at locating and evaluating opportunities in virtual real estate if you have rigorous strategies, a dedication to due diligence, and a combination of inventiveness and tenacity. Welcome to a time when possibilities cross boundaries, properties are evaluated across screens, and your path to successful investing keeps developing.

• Online Resources for Off-Market Deals

Using the Internet to Explore the Digital Goldmine: Finding Off-Market Real Estate Deals

The terrain has changed in the ever changing world of real estate investing, changing how investors find hidden gems outside of the conventional market pathways. The world of online resources for off-market deals, where technology enables investors to avoid the mainstream and delve into a gold mine of unexplored prospects, is the epicenter of this revolutionary transformation. Join us as we negotiate the complexities of online resources for off-market real estate deals, reveal success tactics, and investigate the procedures that result in successful solutions.

Online Resources for Off-Market Deals: Starting the Digital Journey

Finding the Virtual Worlds Hidden Treasures

Imagine a scenario in which you may access unique real estate prospects without being constrained by the restrictions of conventional market channels. In this scenario, technology serves as a link between you and untapped off-market alternatives. Imagine a market where innovative tactics and online tools let you access a sizable collection of properties that aren't listed on public websites. This is the world of internet resources for off-market deals—a setting where strategy and innovation converge to reimagine how investors source assets and unleash unrealized potential.

Online Resources' Influence: Exposing Off-Market Deals

- 1: Wholesaler Platforms: Online wholesaler-specific marketplaces link buyers and sellers of properties not on the open market. Finding offers that are not present on conventional listing websites is made easier by these services.

- 2: Social Media Networks: Online real estate networks on social media platforms allow investors to exchange information on off-market offers, pocket listings, and pre-foreclosure prospects.

- 3. Real estate forums: Online discussion groups for real estate are a goldmine of information and off-market leads. Participate in discussions, ask questions, and get knowledge from seasoned investors who are willing to impart their knowledge.

- 4: Local Networking Groups: Through online gatherings and local networking groups, investors can make connections with like-minded people and exchange knowledge on off-market opportunities nearby.

- 5. Use digital tools to build and execute direct mail campaigns that are specifically aimed at homeowners who could be interested in selling their homes off-market.

- 6: Online auction platforms that feature foreclosed homes and distressed property listings provide investors the chance to purchase off-market deals at attractive pricing.

Success Formulas for Finding Off-Market Deals:

- 1: Establish credibility by keeping an active presence on social media, forums, and real estate sites. Step 1: Create a Strong Online Presence. This presents you as an informed and reliable investor.

- 2: Have Conversations: Take part in internet forums, real estate groups, and conversations. Engaging with the community increases your likelihood of discovering excellent off-market leads.

- 3: Utilize internet data tools to find properties with traits that can indicate a motivation to sell off-market, such as high equity, absentee ownership, or recent divorce filings. Step 3: Leverage Data Analytics.

- 4. Specific marketing initiatives: Create persuasive marketing materials that are specific to homeowners who may be receptive to off-market deals. Email, social media, and even direct mail are all viable methods for distributing these information.

Getting Past Obstacles in Off-Market Deal Sourcing:

- 1: Data Accuracy: Ensure that data obtained from online platforms is accurate. To prevent making decisions based on incorrect or out-of-date information, rely on trustworthy sources and double-check facts.

- 2: Maintaining Competition: Be aware that a variety of investors can access online information. Focus on developing relationships, providing special value, and demonstrating your knowledge if you want to distinguish out.

- 3. Sifting Through Relevant Leads: Not all online leads will be pertinent or appropriate for off-market deals. Spend time carefully vetting leads to make sure they complement your investment approach.

Managing the Virtual Frontier of Off-Market Deals, Conclusion

Remember that technology is your compass, strategy is your guide, and adaptation is your power as you reach the end of this voyage. Accept the benefits of using online platforms to access off-market offers, make the most of digital tools, and navigate the virtual world with skill.

You are at the forefront of a shift in real estate investing that is taking place in pixels, online networks, and data-driven insights. You are well-positioned to succeed in finding off-market real estate bargains because you have rigorous tactics, a dedication to due diligence, a mix of innovation and tenacity, and all of these qualities. Welcome to a time where there are countless options, properties may be found on various screens, and your path to financial success is still developing.

• **Evaluating   Properties Remotely**

Important   Information: Remote   Property Evaluation in the Digital Age

A dramatic change is taking place in the dynamic world of real estate investing, allowing investors to evaluate properties remotely and transcend physical barriers. The technique of remotely analyzing properties, which makes use of technology, data analytics, and virtual tools to make wise investment decisions, represents this paradigm change. Join us on an educational adventure as we delve into the complex world of remotely analyzing properties, reveal success tactics, and investigate the procedures that result in confident and profitable conclusions.

Starting the Remote Expedition: Remote Property Evaluation

The Hidden Meaning of Remote Property Evaluation

Imagine a setting where property evaluations may be completed virtually, where innovation and technology serve as a link between investors and possible investments. Imagine a market where virtual tours, data-driven analysis, and professional insights are all included in distant property evaluations. In this field of remotely analyzing properties, innovation and strategy come together to rethink the entire nature of property evaluation and investment decision-making.

The Influence of Remote Property Assessment:

1: Virtual Property Tours: Use 3D walkthroughs and virtual reality (VR) to remotely tour properties. With the help of these tools, you may virtually examine the design and state of a property for an immersive experience.

2: Online Mapping & Satellite Imagery: Use these resources to evaluate a property's location, nearby amenities, and accessibility to important facilities.

3: Due Diligence in Digital: Conduct in-depth internet research to learn about historical data, property valuations, rental rates, and market trends in your area. Making educated decisions is facilitated by these insights.

4: Engage local experts or virtual assistants to provide insights regarding the state of the property, neighborhood dynamics, and potential difficulties.

5: Online systems that provide detailed information about properties, such as ownership history, tax assessments, and recent sales, are available.

Successful Remote Property Evaluation Techniques:

- Utilize Virtual Tours: Use virtual reality technology to completely immerse yourself in the surroundings of the property. Virtual tours give a thorough idea of the layout and condition of the property.

- Data-Driven Analysis: Examine property valuations, rental demand, and historical trends using online data sources. You can evaluate a property's potential for profitability using data-driven insights.

- Work together with Regional Experts: Make contacts with real estate agents, property managers, or contractors in your area who can examine the property's condition and offer local knowledge.

- Conduct thorough due diligence Do a comprehensive investigation into the ownership, liens, and legal status of the property. In-depth research should be added to remote assessments.

Getting Past Obstacles in Remote Property Evaluation

- Limited Physical Inspection: Be aware of the limitations of remote evaluations, especially when determining the physical condition of a property. Virtual technologies can offer insights, but some things would need to be verified physically.

- Reliability of Data: For your analysis, rely on precise and trustworthy data sources. Verify information from reliable sources to prevent making conclusions based on unreliable or out-of-date data.
- Lack of local knowledge The same amount of expertise of the local market dynamics may not be provided by remote analyses. Working with regional authorities can help close this knowledge gap.

Conclusion: Getting Around the Property Evaluation Digital Horizon

Remember that technology is your compass, strategy is your guide, and adaptation is your strength as this exploration comes to a close. Accept the benefits of remote property evaluation, make use of virtual tools, and navigate the digital environment with skill.

You are at the forefront of this revolution as it occurs in pixels, virtual tours, and data-driven analytics, the future of property appraisal. You are well-positioned to succeed in remotely analyzing properties if you have meticulous strategies, a dedication to due diligence, and a mix of inventiveness and tenacity. Welcome to the era where real estate is viewed across several screens, data-driven insights are gleaned, and your path to making confident investment decisions continues.

Chapter 4: Negotiating and Executing Contracts Virtually

Mastering Virtual Negotiation and Contract Execution: Unlocking Boundless Horizons

A paradigm change of massive proportions has evolved in the constantly changing world of real estate, one in which physical proximity no longer determines the course of discussions and contracts. This game-changing innovation is none other than the art of contract negotiation and execution over the internet—a breakthrough that overcomes geographic boundaries, makes use of technological prowess, and enables investors to negotiate the complex waters of real estate transactions from the comfort of their chosen location. Join us on a thought-provoking journey as we delve into the nuances of online contract execution and negotiation, highlighting its benefits and investigating the procedures that promote successful outcomes.

A Digital Odyssey for Examining the Landscape of Online Contract Negotiation and Execution

Starting a Strategic Virtual Empowerment Journey

Imagine a world where bargaining tables have no boundaries, where contracts are signed electronically rather than in person, and where distance no longer acts as a barrier to the flow of real estate transactions. Imagine a world where technology effortlessly combines with the art of negotiating and contract execution to usher in a new era of real estate transactions. Here, innovation and strategy combine to revolutionize the very nature of real estate discussions. This is the world of virtual negotiation and contract execution.

The benefits of electronic contract execution and negotiation

1: Geographic Independence: Distance barriers are broken during virtual contract negotiations and implementation. The pool of possible partners and deals is widened by the ability of investors to communicate with peers from anywhere in the world.

2: Efficiency Enhanced: Virtual negotiating eliminates the need for lengthy in-person encounters. The speed of communication, the focus of conversations, and the promptness of decisions all help to increase productivity.

3: Enhanced Flexibility: Contract executions and negotiations can be planned to take into account various time zones and timetables. This adaptability makes things more accessible and guarantees efficient operations.

4: Building a Global Network: Virtual negotiation encourages ties outside of local marketplaces. Investors can form partnerships with experts in other locations, expanding their network and presenting new prospects.

5: Cost Savings: Travel and logistics expenses are greatly reduced by virtual contract negotiation and execution. Resources that are saved can be used to improve deal quality or fund key projects.

Compelling Virtual Negotiation and Contract Execution skills

Making Your Virtual Victory Strategy

Techniques for Electronic Contract Negotiation and Execution:

1: Clear Communication: The foundation of online negotiation is effective communication. To ensure debate clarity, use digital communication technologies like email, instant messaging, and video conferencing.

2: Active Listening: During virtual negotiations, it's important to pay close attention to both spoken and unspoken cues. Effective negotiation is facilitated by active listening, which helps to grasp the demands of counterparts.

3: Digital Documentation: Make certain that every agreement, term, and condition is carefully recorded in digital formats. Secure platforms and digital signatures speed up contract execution while maintaining legality.

4: Utilize online negotiation tools created specifically for real estate negotiations. These platforms provide resources for quicker decision-making, document sharing, and group discussions.

Guidelines for Excellence in Virtual Negotiation and Contract Execution

Enhancing Your Virtual Strategy for the Best Results

1: Thorough Preparation: Before negotiations, thoroughly research both parties, the market, and the subject property. Being well-prepared improves your negotiating position.

2: Empathetic Approach: When negotiating online, show some empathy. To customize your approach and achieve a balance, be aware of the viewpoints, motives, and issues of your rivals.

3: Technology Proficiency: Become familiar with systems for contract execution, digital signature programs, and virtual communication tools. The process is streamlined by proficiency with these technologies.

4: Clear Legal Advice: To verify that virtual contracts are valid and enforceable, seek legal counsel. Secure execution requires knowledge of jurisdictional laws and contract specifications.

Conclusion: Getting Around the Digital Success Landscape

You should keep in mind that technology is your ally, strategy is your compass, and adaptability is your strength as you navigate the world of virtual negotiation and contract execution. Accept the benefits of borderless negotiation, take advantage of virtual platforms, and master the digital space.

You are at the forefront of a revolution in real estate negotiation that is taking place in pixels, communication technologies, and virtual signatures. You're prepared to succeed in virtual contract negotiations and execution thanks to your careful planning, strategic thinking, and skillful use of technology and empathy. Welcome to the age of screen-based negotiations and clickable contracts, where your path to virtual negotiating mastery can now begin.

• Effective Virtual Negotiation Techniques

Using Powerful Methods Across Digital Realms: The Art of Virtual Negotiation

In the dynamic world of negotiation, a new domain has developed where conference tables are replaced by screens and debates are guided by individual pixels. This evolution is none other than the mastery of virtual negotiation, a skill that cuts over conventional lines, makes use of technology, and enables negotiators to accomplish their objectives from anywhere in the world. Join us as we explore the practices that lead to success as we delve into the nuances of powerful virtual bargaining strategies, revealing their potency.

Examining the Virtual Negotiation Landscape: A Digital Frontier

Starting a Digital Diplomacy Journey

Imagine a scenario where geographical restrictions no longer limit the range of discussions and virtual environments in place of bargaining tables are the norm. Imagine a world where negotiating skill flourishes behind a screen, where techniques develop alongside technology. This is the virtual negotiating environment, where strategy and innovation come together to rethink what it means to achieve goals through agreements.

The benefits of efficient virtual negotiation strategies include:

1: Global Reach, Local Impact: Global communication is made possible through virtual bargaining, which crosses national boundaries. This global reach increases opportunities while keeping the potency of regional differences.

2: Time and Efficiency: It is impossible to overstate how effective virtual negotiation is. All parties involved benefit from quick communication, succinct debates, and speedy decisions that save them both important time.

3: Negotiations can be organized to take into account various time zones and timetables. Flexibility Unleashed. This adaptability improves accessibility and guarantees smooth operations.

4: Data-driven insights: Virtual discussions are made possible by data analytics, allowing participants to access facts and insights in real-time that guide their strategy.

5: Cost-effective Approach: Virtual bargaining significantly lowers travel and logistical costs. These funds could be used to improve deal quality or to fund strategic initiatives.

Developing Expertise in Virtual Negotiation Methods

Disclosing the Virtual Diplomacy Blueprint

Successful Virtual Negotiation Techniques:

1: Beyond Boundaries: A successful negotiation still depends on thorough preparation. To guide your strategy, investigate market trends, the histories of your competitors, and important details.

2: Virtual empathy is necessary for virtual discussions. Recognize the circumstances, motives, and issues of your counterpart and modify your approach to establish rapport.

3: Effective Communication: To promote clarity and keep lines of communication open, use digital communication technologies like video conferencing, instant messaging, and email.

4: Active Listening: Even in a virtual world, pay close attention to verbal and nonverbal signs. Understanding your counterpart's viewpoint with the use of active listening helps you negotiate more successfully.

The Best Practices for Virtual Negotiation Strategies

Increasing Your Approach for the Best Results

1: Data-Driven Insights: Use data analytics tools to learn more about market trends, property valuations, and other important negotiation-relevant factors. These perceptions provide you a competitive edge.

2: Adaptability is essential in the virtual world. Be ready to adjust your strategy in response to current information and shifting negotiating circumstances.

3: Maintain a Professional Atmosphere: When choosing a virtual setting for discussions, make sure it is distraction-free and exudes professionalism to all sides.

4: Visual Communication: To forge a more intimate relationship, use video conferencing. Body language, facial emotions, and nonverbal cues are still crucial to efficient communication.

Navigating the Digital Frontier of Success, Conclusion

It's important to keep in mind that technology is your ally, strategy is your compass, and adaptability is your strength as you make your way through the world of efficient virtual negotiation strategies. Accept the benefits of borderless negotiation, tap the strength of data-driven insights, and master the art of digital domain navigation.

You are at the forefront of a change in negotiation that is taking place in pixels, virtual spaces, and digital insights. You are well-positioned to succeed in the art of virtual negotiating because you have rigorous plans, a dedication to learning, and a mix of empathy and ingenuity. Welcome to the era of screen-based talks, where deals are sealed with a click, and where your path to mastering virtual negotiations may now begin.

• Remote Contracting and Agreements

Understanding Digital Deal-Making: Navigating the Landscape of Remote Contracting and Agreements

The way contracts and agreements are created has undergone a revolutionary change in the ever-evolving world of business and transactions—a change that transcends geographical boundaries. This transition is none other than the development of remote contracting and agreements—a field in which boundaries of space are blurred, technology is utilized, and the complexities of business negotiations play out across digital environments. Join us as we explore the nuances of remote contracting and agreements, identify their benefits, and reveal the procedures that result in effective solutions.

A Digital Odyssey for Investigating the World of Remote Contracting and Agreements

Setting out on a Virtual Transactions Journey

Imagine a scenario where geographical restrictions no longer affect the timing of agreements and the traditional boardroom has been replaced with a virtual environment. Imagine a world where signing signatures on various digital interfaces is as simple as tapping a keyboard to address legal issues. Here, innovation and law meet to create a new era of deal-making in the world of distant contracts and agreements.

The advantages of remote agreements and contracts:

1: Global Reach, Seamless Communication: Through remote contracting, organizations may make agreements with partners and clients from any location in the world. This international reach expands possibilities while maintaining the core of local cooperation.

2: Efficiency and expediency: It is impossible to overstate how efficient remote contracting is. All parties involved save significant time thanks to prompt communication, real-time contract modifications, and an accelerated procedure.

3: Flexibility and Accessibility: Being able to work remotely gives you more freedom when it comes to scheduling meetings, consultations, and contract signings. This accessibility facilitates collaboration and takes into account various time zones.

4: Paperless Transactions: Remote contracting is naturally green because it reduces the need for paper documents and has a smaller impact on the environment. Paperless transactions also simplify record-keeping and archival processes.

5: Reduced Costs: Remote contracting significantly lowers related costs by avoiding the need for physical travel and substantial documentation. These funds may be used for more strategic projects.

Developing Your Remote Contracting and Agreements Craft

Techniques for Agreements and Remote Contracting:

1: Employ systems for digital documentation that let people create, share, and collaborate on contracts. Real-time updates and modifications are made possible by these systems, ensuring that everyone is on the same page.

2: Electronic Signatures: Use reliable and secure technologies for electronic signatures. Platforms that allow signatories to add their digital signatures quickly and easily expedite the execution procedure.

3: Use video conferencing software to conduct meetings, discussions, and negotiations. Even in a digital context, video communication creates connection and increases engagement.

4: Secure Communication routes: When transferring sensitive contract and agreement-related information, pick secure communication routes. The confidentiality of data must be protected at all costs.

Best Practices for Contracts and Remote Work that Succeed

Enhancing Your Digital Strategy for the Best Results

1: Complete and understandable contract documentation that outlines the terms, conditions, and responsibilities of all parties is required. Successful distant agreements depend on clear documentation.

2: Legal Knowledge: To verify that distant contracts are valid and enforceable, get legal counsel. Legal professionals can offer advice on jurisdictional laws and particular terms that apply to remote transactions.

3: Prioritize digital platform security when it comes to contracting and agreement execution. Ascertain that data is encrypted and secured against possible breaches.

4: Clearly defined channels of communication should be established with each party to the agreement. To keep communication open and prevent misunderstandings, respond to any queries or concerns right away.

Conclusion: Understanding the Digital Transaction Horizon

Always keep in mind that technology is your ally, legality is your compass, and adaptability is your strength as you negotiate the world of remote contracting and agreements. Adopt the benefits of borderless deal-making, utilize the strength of digital signatures, and navigate the digital environment with skill.

You're at the forefront of a shift in contracting and agreements that is taking place in pixels, electronic signatures, and secure platforms. You are ready to succeed in the realm of remote contracting and agreements if you have meticulous strategies, a dedication to legality, and a balance of innovation and diligence. Welcome to the era of digital deal-making, where agreements are made across screens and contracts are signed with a single click.

Chapter 5: Closing Virtual Wholesaling Deals

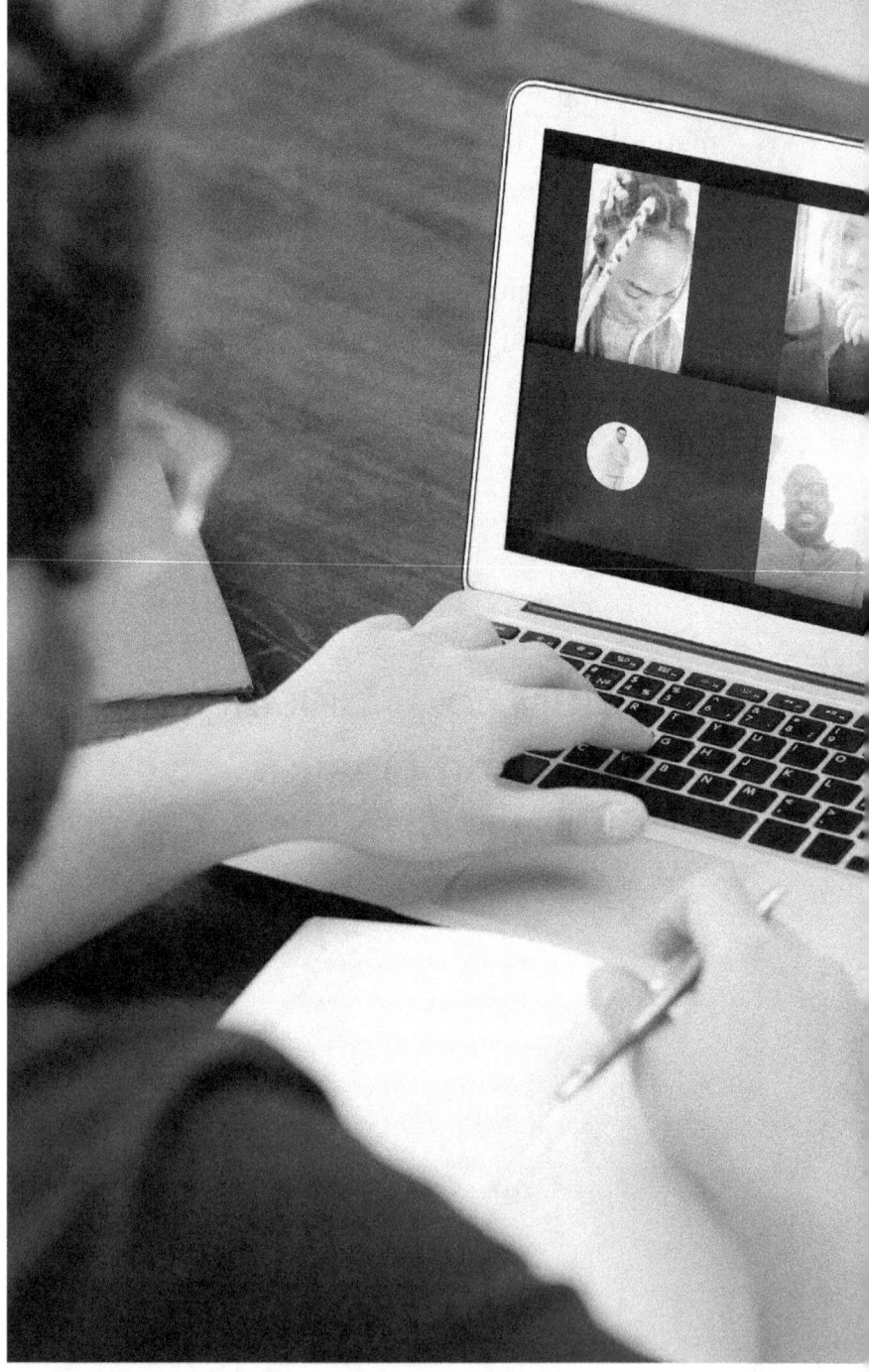

The Art of Closing Virtual Wholesaling Deals: Finding Your Way to Success

A new frontier has opened up in the fast-paced world of real estate—a place where properties are traded, agreements are signed, and transactions are completed virtually. This revolutionary aspect is none other than the skill of finishing virtual wholesaling deals—a strategy that transcends geographic boundaries, makes use of technological innovation, and equips investors to successfully negotiate the complex process of closing deals from any location on Earth. Join us on an insightful journey as we delve into the nuances of concluding virtual wholesaling deals, reveal the success-driven tactics, and investigate the procedures that produce successful outcomes.

A Digital Odyssey for Investigating the Landscape of Closing Virtual Wholesaling Deals

Starting a Remote Transaction Mastery Journey

Imagine a setting where the rules of proximity no longer govern the flow of real estate transactions—a setting where discussions take place virtually, contracts are signed electronically, and deals are finalized without the requirement of an in-person closing. Imagine a market where creativity and business acumen combine to reinvent the very nature of real estate wholesaling. The realm of virtual wholesale sales is one where opportunities are maximized, efficiency is improved, and transactions go beyond the bounds of conventional business.

The Benefits of Completing Online Wholesaling Deals:

1: Global Reach, Local Impact: By concluding virtual wholesaling agreements, investors can gain access to properties in numerous marketplaces without being physically present. The benefit of local expertise and insights is combined with this global viewpoint.

2: Speed and Efficiency: The speed and efficiency of virtual deal closing are unmatched. Documents are shared electronically, processes are expedited, and the total transaction time is drastically reduced.

3. Reduced expenses: The need for lengthy travel is essentially eliminated when transactions are closed, which lowers associated expenses and frees up funds to improve deal quality or grow the organization.

4: Flexibility and Accessibility: Because deal closure takes place virtually, accessibility and scheduling flexibility are also possible. Regardless of time zones or location, parties can work together and complete transactions.

5: Paperless Transactions: By reducing the usage of physical paperwork, the shift to virtual deal closure promotes an environmentally responsible philosophy. Digital records and archives also improve record-keeping and organizing.

Understanding of Virtual Wholesaling Deals Closing

Developing Your Remote Success Strategy

Methods for Sealing Deals in Virtual Wholesaling:

1: Digital Documentation: Share, sign, and exchange documentation through digital platforms. Real-time updates and revisions are made possible via electronic signatures and secure document sharing services.

2: Utilize video conferencing equipment for conversations, negotiations, and consults. Even in a virtual setting, video communication increases engagement and develops a sense of connection.

3: Secure Communication methods: When transferring private information such as contract terms, pricing, and deal details, use secure communication methods. Security of data is crucial.

4: Legal Advice: To ensure the validity and enforceability of virtual transactions, seek legal counsel. Legal professionals can advise on jurisdictional laws and particular terms that apply to distant dealings.

Guidelines for Closing Virtual Wholesaling Deals at the Highest Level

Increasing Your Strategy for the Best Results

1: Extensive Due Diligence: Extensive due diligence should be done on the property, market conditions, and counterparts' backgrounds. A solid knowledge base allows self-assurance and success in virtual transactions.

2: Communication and Transparency: Keep the lines of communication open with all parties to the transaction. In order to maintain openness and prevent misunderstandings, swiftly respond to all inquiries, worries, and updates.

3: Digital Security: Give priority to the safety of online platforms used to close deals. To protect sensitive information, be sure that data is encrypted and that privacy safeguards are in place.

4: Utilize digital marketing strategies to draw in motivated vendors and prospective purchasers. To increase your reach and produce leads, make use of social media, email campaigns, and internet platforms.

Managing the Virtual Frontier of Deal Closing, Conclusion

Always keep in mind that technology is your ally, strategy is your compass, and adaptability is your strength as you navigate the realm of closing virtual wholesaling agreements. Accept the benefits of borderless commerce, leverage the strength of digital documentation, and navigate the digital environment with skill.

You're at the forefront of this shift as the future of real estate deal closing is being shaped by pixels, electronic signatures, and secure platforms. You are well-positioned to succeed in closing virtual wholesaling sales if you have meticulous tactics, a dedication to transparency, and a balance of creativity and assiduity. Welcome to the age of digital deal-closing prowess, where transactions are completed across screens and agreements are executed with a single click.

- **Virtual Closing Procedures and Challenges**

Virtual Closing Procedures and Overcoming Challenges: Navigating the Digital Nexus

A revolutionary paradigm has emerged in the constantly changing real estate market—one in which closing deals, executing transactions, and transferring property all take place online. This change is at the core of virtual closing processes, a strategy that breaks down geographical barriers, leverages digital platforms, and equips investors to successfully complete deals remotely. Join us on an educational journey as we examine the nuances of virtual closure procedures, identify the difficulties they present, and consider solutions.

A Digital Odyssey for Investigating the World of Virtual Closing Procedures

Setting out on a Remote Culmination Journey

Imagine a scenario in which the completion of real estate transactions is no longer governed by physical proximity; instead, documents are transferred with the click of a button, and signatures are attached across digital interfaces. Imagine a world without conventional restrictions, where property ownership transfers happen fluidly between screens. The world of virtual closing processes is one in which innovation and utility reinvent the fundamentals of concluding real estate deals.

Virtual Closing Procedures' Benefits:

1: Local knowledge with a global reach: Investors can finish deals in a variety of markets thanks to virtual closing procedures that cut through geographical boundaries. This global viewpoint is strengthened by local knowledge, resulting in a potent synthesis of insights.

2: Enhanced Efficiency Virtual closure has unsurpassed effectiveness. Documents are electronically transferred, processes are expedited, and the entire transaction's schedule is drastically reduced.

3: Cost Effectiveness: By removing the need for considerable travel and logistics, virtual closure lowers associated expenses. This makes it possible to allocate resources to boosting deal quality or growing the investment portfolio.

4:The virtual nature of closing procedures provides unmatched flexibility, as well as accessibility. Regardless of time zones or locations, parties can communicate, exchange papers, and finalize transactions.

5: Improved Record-Keeping: The switch to virtual closing encourages organized and effective record-keeping. Digital archives simplify post-closing procedures and allow for quick access to documentation.

Knowing how to use virtual closing procedures

Developing Your Remote Success Strategy

Successful Virtual Closing Procedures: Strategies

1: Platforms for digital documentation that allow for the sharing, signing, and exchange of documents should be adopted. The process is streamlined by electronic signatures and safe document sharing.

2. Remote Notarization: Use online notarization services when it's legal to do so. By using this method, remote practices are followed while ensuring that documents are notarized.

3: Secure Communication Channels: Give secure communication channels a priority when transferring sensitive information on contract execution, financial information, and deal terms. Security of data is crucial.

4: Establish open channels of communication with all stakeholders concerned with the closure process. To ensure transparency, respond as soon as possible to inquiries, worries, and updates.

Getting Past Obstacles in Virtual Closing Processes

Techniques for Avoiding Potential Obstacles

1: Legal Compliance: It is crucial to make sure that virtual closing procedures abide by local legal requirements and regulations. To confirm the validity and enforceability of distant transactions, consult legal counsel.

2: Document Authenticity: Address security and authenticity concerns concerning documents by using secure digital platforms and legally enforceable electronic signatures.

3: Technological Literacy: Some parties to the transaction might not be used to online transactions. Offer assistance and support for utilizing digital channels.

4: Utilize secure channels, communicate using encryption, and adhere to data privacy laws to protect sensitive information.

Managing the Virtual Frontier of Closings, Conclusion

Keep in mind that technology is your ally, compliance is your compass, and adaptation is your strength as you navigate the world of virtual closing procedures. Accept the benefits of borderless commerce, leverage the strength of digital documentation, and navigate the digital environment with skill.

You are at the forefront of a shift in real estate closing that is taking place in secure platforms, electronic signatures, and pixels. You are prepared to succeed in the field of virtual closing procedures with careful tactics, a dedication to legal compliance, and a balance of creativity and diligence. Welcome to a time when transactions are completed across screens, ownership is changed with a single click, and your path to mastering digital closings is just beginning.

• Ensuring a Smooth Remote Transaction

Making Remote Real Estate Transactions Seamless: Navigating Smooth Waters

A new vista has opened up in the dynamic world of real estate—a world where agreements are made, contracts are exchanged, and deals are closed through the internet. This revolutionary paradigm shift is none other than the art of facilitating a seamless remote transaction—a strategy that transcends geographical borders, makes use of the power of digital technology, and equips investors to successfully negotiate the treacherous waters of real estate transactions from any location on Earth. Join us on a discovery journey as we delve into the nuances of guaranteeing smooth remote transactions, reveal success techniques, and investigate the behaviors that result in successful outcomes.

A Digital Odyssey for Examining the Landscape of Simple Remote Transactions

Setting off on a Path of Transaction Excellence

Imagine a situation in which physical presence is not required to complete transactions; instead, negotiations would be done via digital interfaces, documents would be exchanged with the press of a button, and ownership of properties would be transferred without it. Imagine a world where deal-making is shaped by technology and transactional elegance flourishes within the boundaries of screens. This is the world of seamless remote transactions, where innovation and strategy come together to reimagine how real estate deals go through the process.

The advantages of making sure remote transactions go smoothly

1: Local Focus, Global Reach: Making sure remote transactions go smoothly gives investors access to properties and possibilities in several markets. The knowledge of local specialists complements this global reach.

2: Speed and Efficiency: Remote transactions have the highest level of efficiency. Rapid document interchange, prompt communication, and a drastically reduced schedule are all benefits.

3: Lower Costs: By removing the need for lengthy travel, remote transactions lower the costs involved. These resources could be used to improve deal quality or fund key projects.

4: Flexibility and Accessibility: Because remote transactions are virtual, they are flexible in terms of scheduling and accessibility. No matter where they are located in the world or in what time zone, parties can work together, share papers, and complete transactions.

5: Improved Record-Keeping: The switch to remote transactions makes record-keeping and organizing more effective. Access to paperwork and post-transaction procedures are made easier by digital archives.

Understanding of Smoothing Out Remote Transactions

Developing Your Remote Success Strategy

Successful Remote Transaction Techniques:

1: Digital Documentation Platforms: Make use of safe digital platforms for collaboration, document signing, and sharing. The transaction procedure is streamlined via electronic signatures and secure document exchange.

2: Utilize video conferencing capabilities for virtual negotiations, talks, and consultations (optional). In a remote setting, visual communication creates connection and increases engagement.

3. Clearly Express Yourself Establish direct channels of communication with all participants

to the transaction. Transparency and productive collaboration are enhanced by frequent updates and rapid responses.

4: Legal Advice: To assure the validity and enforceability of remote transactions, consult a lawyer. Legal professionals can advise on jurisdictional laws and specific terms.

Recommended Practices for Smooth Remote Transactions

Increasing Your Strategy for the Best Results

1: Extensive Due Diligence: Extensive due diligence should be done on the property, the backgrounds of the counterparts, and market trends. A solid knowledge base boosts self-assurance and success in distant transactions.

2: Maintain structured digital documents throughout the transaction process with step number two, document management. Having centralized files and records improves productivity and accessibility.

3: Data Security: Give top priority to protecting digital platforms used for exchanging documents and conducting business transactions. Use secure channels and encryption to protect sensitive data.

4: Collaborative Approach: Promote a collaborative atmosphere by keeping lines of communication open and swiftly responding to inquiries and concerns. The success of a transaction is influenced by a sense of partnership.

The Virtual Frontier of Transaction Excellence: Exploring it in Conclusive

Always keep in mind that technology is your ally, strategy is your compass, and adaptability is your strength as you traverse the world of assuring successful remote transactions. Embrace the benefits of global business dealing, make the most of digital documents, and navigate the digital environment with skill.

You are at the forefront of a shift in real estate transactions that is taking place in secure platforms, digital communication, and pixels. You are well-positioned to succeed in providing seamless remote transactions with careful planning, a dedication to legal compliance, and a balance of creativity and caution. Welcome to the era where transactions take place across screens and contracts are signed with a single click. Your path to becoming an expert in remote transactions can now begin.

Chapter 6: Scaling and Future of Virtual Wholesaling

The Future of Virtual Wholesaling and Scaling: A Future Roadmap

A new chapter is being written in the dynamic world of real estate, one that pushes the limits of conventional methods, makes use of cutting-edge technology, and paves the way for unheard-of expansion. This groundbreaking section is none other than the future of virtual wholesaling—a field where innovation and strategy come together to fundamentally alter how properties are found, deals are sealed, and businesses are scaled. Come along on an exploration voyage with us as we explore the complexities of expanding virtual wholesaling, identify the benefits and problems it brings, and imagine a time in the future where boundaries are blurred and possibilities are limitless.

A Digital Odyssey for Unveiling the Future of Virtual Wholesaling

Starting a Journey of Evolution and Growth

Imagine a future in which geographic restrictions do not limit your capacity to find assets, form alliances, and increase your real estate portfolio. Imagine a world where technology is used to increase your virtual wholesaler reach, efficiency, and effectiveness. This is the field of virtual wholesaling's future, one in which innovation advances your company and transforms how you handle real estate deals.

Scaling Virtual Wholesaling's Potential:

1: Local Skill, Global Reach: Scaling virtual wholesaling gives you the ability to access a variety of global markets. Your business can operate internationally while benefiting from local knowledge's insights.

2. Efficiency Amplified: You may simplify your operations, from property identification through deal closure, by utilizing technology and digital technologies. Gains in efficiency are multiplied, increasing transaction flow and income.

3: Reduced Overhead: You can control overhead expenses as you grow your online wholesaling business. Financial sustainability is improved by getting rid of physical offices and cutting back on travel-related costs.

4: Utilizing Data: As you scale, data analytics and market insights become your partners. You may spot patterns, focus on high-potential regions, and hone your tactics by using data-driven decision-making.

5: Automated Workflows: The opportunity to implement automated workflows increases with scalability. Automation guarantees consistent and effective operations for everything from lead generation to contact with partners and customers.

Future-Proofing Techniques for Growing Virtual Wholesaling

Leading the Way to Expansion

Scaling Techniques for Online Wholesaling

1: Technology Integration: Invest in technological infrastructure that supports online wholesale business. These solutions, which range from virtual deal negotiating platforms to customer relationship management (CRM) systems, serve as the foundation for your expanding initiatives.

2. Team Building: As your firm grows, think about putting together a virtual team that can handle different facets of it, such lead generation, negotiations, and contract management. Hire professionals in related industries to strengthen your abilities.

3. Outsourcing: By contracting out non-core duties like marketing and administration, you'll have more time for high-value activities like deal analysis and networking.

4: Standardize your processes and record the best practices, which is step four. This constancy makes sure that even as your company grows, your quality will not be affected.

Scaling Virtual Wholesaling: Navigating Opportunities and Challenges

Techniques for Surmounting Challenges and Embracing Potential

1. Conduct rigorous market research as you expand into new markets to understand the dynamics, demand, and competition in each area.

2: Conforming to Regulations: Local laws can differ greatly from those in other areas. To avoid potential hazards, it's crucial to become familiar with local rules and regulations.

3. Upholding Quality: As your volume increases, it's critical to maintain the quality of your products and services. Maintain your reputation for providing value by aiming for consistency in your business practices.

4. Relationship-Building: While technology is important, real estate remains primarily a people business. Work to build rapport and trust with partners, vendors, and customers.

Future-Proofing: A Vision for Virtual Wholesaling

Predicting the Industry's Evolution

1: Virtual Reality Integration: In the future, property tours and inspections may be conducted in virtual reality (VR). Virtual property tours allowed buyers to better comprehend and make decisions.

2: Blockchain technology has the potential to simplify contract execution and record-keeping. Once certain criteria are met, smart contracts would automatically carry out their terms.

3: AI-Driven Predictive Analysis: With the ability to forecast market trends and property values, artificial intelligence could help distributors make more educated decisions.

4: Global Collaboration: As technology fills in the gaps left by distance and time zones, virtual wholesalers may work in creative joint ventures with investors and partners around the world.

The Future of Virtual Wholesaling: Navigating It

Be sure to keep in mind that innovation is your road map, strategy is your compass, and adaptability is your strength as you set out on the path to scale your online wholesaling firm. Take advantage of borderless expansion, maximize the potential of digital platforms, and master the virtual world.

You are at the forefront of a shift in virtual wholesaling that is taking place in pixels, technology integration, and cross-border linkages. You are well-positioned to succeed in scaling virtual wholesaling if you have detailed tactics, a dedication to perfection, a mix of invention and tenacity, and all of these qualities. Welcome to the era where transactions take place across screens, opportunities abound, and your path to successful virtual wholesaling is developing.

• Scaling Your Virtual Wholesaling Business

Scaling Your Virtual Wholesaling Business: Exploring Digital Growth

A tremendous change has taken place in the dynamic world of real estate, one that pushes the limits of conventional property transactions and embraces the possibilities of technological innovation. This game-changing phenomena is none other than the art of scaling a virtual wholesaling company—a venture that overcomes geographic limitations, makes use of technology, and enables investors to scale their businesses in previously unheard-of ways. Come along on an exploration voyage with us as we explore the complexities of growing a virtual wholesale business, identify the keys to success, and confront the difficulties of expansion in the digital era.

Path of Scaling: A Digital Odyssey, Starting Out

Sailing into the Digital Growth Horizon

Imagine a situation in which the constraints of physical presence no longer limit the range of your real estate endeavors—a situation in which properties are sought after, agreements are made, and alliances are formed from the comfort of digital places. Imagine a market where technology is used to expand your reach, innovation drives growth, and scaling your virtual wholesaling company is a reality. The world of scaling in the digital era is one in which options are limitless and where expansion has no national or territorial limitations.

The Benefits of Growing Your Online Wholesaling Company:

1: Local knowledge with a global reach: You gain the ability to enter a variety of marketplaces throughout the world by growing your virtual wholesaling business. You can grow your business well beyond your initial footprint while utilizing the insights of local experts.

2: Operational Efficiency: As your business grows, technology can help you streamline procedures. Digital technologies improve efficiency and let you handle a higher volume of transactions, from lead creation to deal completion.

3: Reduced Overhead: By removing geographical restrictions, you can spend less on things like office space, transportation, and logistics. This effectiveness results in lower overhead expenses.

4: Decision-Making Supported by Data: Scaling demands making wise decisions. Analyzing market circumstances, spotting trends, and optimizing your strategy for maximum impact all depend on data analytics.

5: Automated Workflows: As your firm grows, automation becomes crucial. Automated processes allow you to focus on high-value tasks while ensuring consistency.

Developing Your Scalable Business Plan for Virtual Wholesaling

Leading the Way to Expansion

Successful Scaling Strategies:

1: Utilize digital tools by making an investment in software that supports online wholesaling activities. These tools serve as the foundation for your growth, from deal analysis software to customer relationship management (CRM) systems.

2. Create a Virtual Team: As your firm grows, think about putting together a virtual team with

members who have expertise in various areas. Your competencies can be strengthened by working with professionals in lead generation, negotiations, and other fields.

3. Outsource Non-Core Functions: By outsourcing non-core administrative, marketing, and other responsibilities, you can devote more of your time to high-impact pursuits like deal analysis and networking.

4: Establish consistent processes and record best practices. This is step four of standardizing processes. With standardization, you can handle higher volumes without sacrificing quality.

Managing Obstacles and Taking Advantage of Opportunities

Techniques for Surmounting Challenges and Embracing Potential

Challenges:

1. Conduct rigorous market research as you enter new markets to comprehend regional dynamics, demand, and competition. Every market has particular difficulties that call for careful thought.

2: Regional Differences in Regulations: Regulations vary from one location to another. Learn the local rules and ordinances that apply to real estate transactions in order to ensure compliance.

3. Quality Maintenance: It's essential to keep your deals and services at a high standard as you grow. To protect your reputation and the integrity of your brand, put strict quality control methods in place.

4: Building relationships continues to be important, even when technology is a tool. To manage the complexity of real estate, cultivate trust and rapport with buyers, sellers, and partners.

Leading the Way for Virtual Wholesaling in the Future

Imagining the Development of the Sector

Trends to Watch as Virtual Wholesaling Scales:

1: Advanced Data Analytics: Improved data analytics and predictive modeling will allow virtual wholesalers to make decisions based on data that produce the best results.

2: Blockchain and Smart Contracts: Blockchain technology offers efficiency, security, and transparency, which could change contract execution and record-keeping.

3. The use of virtual reality (VR) could change property tours and inspections, enabling purchasers to research properties from a distance and make educated judgments.

4: Global Collaboration: As a result of technological development, virtual wholesalers will be able to create partnerships and joint ventures on a global scale.

The Future of Virtual Wholesaling: Navigating It

Be sure to keep in mind that innovation is your compass, strategy is your guide, and adaptability is your strength as you set sail on the quest to scale your online wholesaling firm. Accept the benefits of borderless expansion, make the most of digital technologies, and master the digital environment.

You are set to lead this change of virtual wholesaling as it develops in pixels, technological integration, and global connectivity. You are prepared to succeed in growing your online wholesaling business if you have rigorous strategies, a dedication to quality, and a balance of innovation and tenacity. Welcome to the modern day, where growth knows no bounds, contracts are signed on screens, and your path to successful virtual wholesaling keeps developing.

• Trends and Innovations in Virtual Real Estate Transactions

Trends and Innovations in Virtual Real Estate Transactions: Charting the Future

A transformational tidal is rolling across the dynamic real estate market, transforming the way homes are bought, sold, and traded. The trends and breakthroughs in virtual real estate transactions are the source of this revolutionary wave—an movement that embraces technology, reimagines conventional methods, and unlocked new levels of accessibility and efficiency. Join us as we delve into the nuances of virtual real estate transactions, uncover the trends propelling this revolution, and investigate the innovations that are influencing the industry's future.

Virtual Horizon Exploration: A Digital Odyssey

Starting a Transformational Journey

Imagine living in a society where being able to deal in real estate is no longer restricted by geographical bounds. In this scenario, it is possible to tour homes online, have negotiations online, and sign contracts using convenient digital interfaces. Imagine a market where technology is used to improve the transaction experience and where innovation and strategy converge to change the fundamentals of real estate transactions. The future of the industry is being rewritten in the world of virtual real estate transactions, where possibilities are endless.

Trends Supporting Transactions in Virtual Real Estate:

1: Property tours are being revolutionized by virtual reality (VR) and augmented reality (AR). Now that prospective purchasers may view properties electronically, they can make well-informed judgments while saving time and resources.

2: Digital Due Diligence: Before making a purchase, consumers can undertake thorough due diligence thanks to online research tools and data analytics. By arming consumers with knowledge, this tendency improves transparency.

3. Remote Contract Execution: Digital contracts and electronic signatures are increasingly frequent. Remote contract execution speeds up the transaction process by allowing parties to complete agreements without being physically present.

4: Online Listing Platforms: Real estate listings are now available on websites that include in-depth details, images, and videos. This pattern increases exposure and enables buyers to narrow down properties based on particular requirements.

5: Blockchain and Smart Contracts: Blockchain technology has the ability to completely transform real estate transactions. Smart contracts reduce the need for middlemen and increase security by automating and validating agreements.

Future-Shaping Innovations

1: Blockchain can improve the security and usability of title records, lowering fraud and speeding up the transfer of property ownership.

2: Predictive Analytics: Advanced data analytics and artificial intelligence enable predictive modeling, which enables investors to more precisely estimate property prices and discover possible investment hotspots.

3. Chatbot Integration: Virtual assistants and chatbots are being used to book virtual tours, answer questions about properties, and perform other customer service-related tasks.

4: Lenders are embracing digital platforms for mortgage approvals, streamlining the application process and speeding loan decisions. This brings us to point number four: digital mortgage approvals.

Choosing Between the Benefits and Challenges

Taking Advantage of Chances and Avoiding Obstacles

1: Benefits of Online Real Estate Transactions 1 Accessibility: Because virtual transactions are not restricted by physical distance, both buyers and sellers can enter into agreements.

2: Efficiency: Both buyers and sellers benefit from the shortened procedures of virtual transactions, which save time. Digital document exchange, signing, and sharing can cut down on paper effort and administrative red tape.

3: Transparency: Digital tools make it possible to make informed selections by providing detailed information about properties and market trends.

4: Cost Reduction: Virtual transactions reduce travel and related expenses, freeing up funds to improve the quality of negotiations.

5: Safety and Convenience: Virtual transactions support company continuity while putting safety and convenience first, which is especially important during times of crisis.

Challenges in Transacting in Virtual Real Estate:

1: Technological Literacy: There may be a learning curve associated with using digital technologies because not all stakeholders are likely to be equally accustomed to them.

2: Security Issues: Security concerns are raised by the digital world, especially when dealing with private and sensitive financial and personal data.

3. Regulatory Obstacles: Regulations governing virtual transactions can be difficult to understand and may differ from one jurisdiction to another.

4. Loss of Personal Touch: The lack of face-to-face encounters may lessen the personal touch, which is important for establishing rapport and trust.

To sum up: Accepting the Virtual Future

Remember that technology is your ally, strategy is your compass, and flexibility is your strength as you negotiate the world of virtual real estate deals. Take advantage of borderless commerce's advantages, tap the potential of digital innovation, and navigate the virtual world with skill.

You are at the forefront of a shift in real estate transactions that is being shaped by pixels, blockchain integration, and predictive analytics. You are well-positioned to succeed in the realm of virtual real estate transactions with careful planning, a dedication to excellence, and a combination of ingenuity and tenacity. Welcome to a time when transactions take place across several screens, real estate may be viewed in virtual reality, and the potential for success is limitless.

- **What to Say and What Not to Say**

What to Say and What Not to Say When Mastering the Art of Virtual Wholesaling

The real estate market is being revolutionized by virtual wholesaling, which gives investors the chance to take advantage of technology and reach previously unreachable regions. Effective communication is just as important for this industry's success as technology is. When buying and selling real estate electronically, knowing what to say and what not to say might mean the difference between a successful business and missed possibilities. In this in-depth manual, we'll examine the art of communication in virtual wholesaling, emphasizing the crucial words and tactics that are effective and outlining the pitfalls to avoid.

What to Say in Part 1

Creating a relationship with sellers

1: Welcome and introduction
A friendly and professional greeting when making first contact with a potential seller establishes the tone for the conversation.

Greeting them with something like, "Hello, my name is [Your Name], and I'm interested in discussing your property," is an excellent place to start.

2: Demonstrating Interest

Declare your real interest in the seller's property. Possibly say something along the lines of, "I've heard great things about your property, and I'd love to learn more." to pique interest.

3. Recognizing the needs of the seller

Equally important to talking is listening in effective communication. To better grasp the needs and goals of the seller, provide open-ended inquiries like, "What motivated you to consider selling your property?"

4: Benefits of Working with You

Describe the advantages of cooperating with you to the seller. To demonstrate your expertise and experience, say something like, "I have a proven track record of successful transactions and can make the selling process hassle-free for you."

5. **Bargaining and Offers**

Clarity is essential in negotiations and offer-making. Say something along the lines of "I'd like to discuss the terms of our potential agreement, including the offer I can make on your property."

Getting in touch with customers

1: **Property Descriptions**

Write captivating property descriptions that emphasize the property's distinctive attributes. Take the statement, "This property boasts a spacious, sunlit living room with panoramic views."

2: **Price haggling**

Maintain professionalism and compassion throughout price negotiations. Invoke the phrase

"Let's work together to find a price that works for both of us."

3. Transaction Information

Potential buyers should be well informed of the transactional procedure. "This is how the purchasing process works, step by step," said.

Partnering and Networking

1: Introduction and Cooperation

Whenever you contact prospective investors or partners, make a professional introduction. "I'm [Your Name], and I'm interested in investigating potential cooperative ventures in the real estate market," you should say.

2: Presenting Win-Win Case Studies

Promote cooperation as a win-win situation. I think we can build a win-win situation that maximizes our returns if we work together, so say that.

Advertising and marketing

1: **Making marketing messages**

Create persuasive marketing messages that speak to your target market. Think about the phrase "Discover your dream home with our exclusive property listings."

2:

Select the best internet platforms to successfully reach your audience. Suggest something along the lines of, "Our properties are listed on reputable online platforms to ensure maximum visibility."

Conflict Resolution and Problem-Solving

1: **handling difficult situations**

When conflicts emerge, handle them in a professional manner. You may say something like, "I understand your worries, and I'm open to finding a solution that works for both parties."

2: **Keeping Professionalism**

No matter what, always speak in a formal manner. Express your gratitude for the feedback and your commitment to having the situation resolved to your satisfaction.

What Not to Say in Part 2

Creating a relationship with sellers

1. Overpromising
Don't make grandiose promises. Instead of stating that "I guarantee your property will sell within a week," offer instead that "I'll work diligently to sell your property as quickly as possible."

2. Pushing the Seller
Observe the seller's schedule. Be careful not to apply pressure, such as saying, "You must decide now, or this offer won't be available."

3. Harsh Language
Maintain a confident and expert demeanor. Stay away from critical remarks like, "This property needs a lot of work."

Getting in touch with customers

1: Representing the Property Falsely

Give precise details regarding the property. Do not assert untrue statements such as "This property has never had any issues."

2: Making hollow promises

Regarding what you can give, be sincere. Don't state, "You'll make a fortune with this investment," instead add, "This investment has the potential for significant returns."

Partnering and Networking

1: Being excessively egocentric

Focus on shared benefits rather than just your individual benefit. You should refrain from saying things like, "I'm only interested in what I can get out of this."

Advertising and marketing

1: False advertising

Respect advertising laws and steer clear of dishonest marketing techniques. Saying things such as, "Get rich quick with our properties," which are untrue, should be replaced with, "Explore investment opportunities with us."

Conflict Resolution and Problem-Solving

1: **Conflicts that escalate**

Before increasing disputes, try to find a solution. Avoid using threatening language such as, "I'll sue if you don't comply."

2: Keeping Professionalism

Maintain professionalism even in difficult circumstances. Describe your commitment to finding a solution that pleases all sides by saying, "I value your feedback."

Conclusion

The foundation of virtual wholesaling success is effective communication. Building trust, fostering healthy connections, and navigating the difficulties of real estate transactions in the digital sphere may all be facilitated by understanding what to say and what not to say. In the realm of online wholesaling, improving your communication skills can help you build credibility, grow your network, and accomplish your objectives

Conclusion:

Developing the Real Estate Transactions of the Future Online

We've set out on a fascinating expedition as we navigate the dynamic world of virtual real estate transactions—a journey that has revealed the intricate details of an industry revolution. As our investigation comes to a close, it is clear that the real estate industry is going through a change unlike anything else. Future borders will be blurred, opportunities will be limitless, and the whole nature of real estate transactions will change as a result of the integration of technology, innovation, and strategy.

A Vision Realized: The Development of Virtual Real Estate Transactions

- Since the beginning of this voyage, we have observed the development of a period—a world in which properties can be toured electronically, transactions can be carried out remotely, and blockchain technology is reinventing the very basis of real estate ownership. This progression represents a paradigm change that marks the maturation of an industry that has embraced the possibilities of the digital age, not merely a collection of trends.

The Power of Innovation and Technology: Considering the Future

- On this trip, technology and innovation have served as our guides, revealing a route that results in increased effectiveness, accessibility, and transparency. We can now experience realistic, time- and space-free property tours thanks to virtual reality (VR), which has helped us transcend geographical boundaries. A glimpse into a future where smart contracts speed transactions and tamper-proof title records are possible has been provided by the way that blockchain technology has changed the rules of security and trust.

Navigating Difficulties: Turning Roadblocks Into Opportunities

- We have had difficulties along the way, as with any transforming journey. Obstacles include the requirement for computer knowledge, security-related worries, and legislative specifics of the digital sphere. Nevertheless, these difficulties have encouraged innovation and expansion. In order to prepare the way for a safer, more seamless future, they have inspired the sector to reinvent solutions, support security measures, and interact with regulatory organizations.

Future Unleashed: A Landscape of Possibilities

- We are presented with a vista of limitless opportunity when we look toward the future. Artificial intelligence and predictive analytics have the potential to improve investment choices by providing information that could change the course of the sector itself. Virtual assistants and chatbots are prepared to reinvent client engagement by offering round-the-clock assistance. Virtual reality could alter how purchasers see possible homes, enabling them to make judgments with greater certainty and accuracy.

The journey continues as you take part in the digital revolution.

- Your trip in the world of virtual real estate transactions is far from over as this exploration comes to a close. You are prepared to be a trailblazer in a future where the distinction between the physical and digital worlds is blurred because you have insights, strategies, and a grasp of the trends and technologies driving this shift. Your success in a world where the digital environment coexists with the concrete field of real estate depends on your capacity to adapt, perseverance, and willingness to embrace change.

A Dream Fulfilled: Setting Your Course

You've discovered the promise of virtual real estate transactions with each step you've taken on this journey—the potential to cross boundaries, increase efficiency, and promote transparency. You are well-equipped to negotiate the always changing landscape of virtual real estate transactions because you have knowledge of trends, insights into difficulties, and a vision of advancements.

Remember that technology is your ally, innovation is your compass, and adaptability is your strength as you plot your future course. The future is here: a future in which transactions take place across screens, in which buyers view properties through virtual reality headsets, and in which the potential of the digital age transforms the very foundations of real estate.

Welcome to the vanguard of the virtual revolution, a future in which opportunities are endless, innovation drives progress, and you play a leading role in the thrilling development of virtual real estate deals.